SHAVING STROKES

SHAVING STROKES
by Frank Beard
Illustrations by Murray Olderman

Cover Photo Courtesy of Golf Magazine

GROSSET & DUNLAP
A NATIONAL GENERAL COMPANY

Publishers   New York

CONTENTS

IV. THE WOODS

V. STROKE SAVERS

VI. FINE POINTS

SHAVING STROKES

GETTING
IN THE GROOVE

GETTING
IN THE GROOVE

☐After three or four months winter hibernation, no sensible golfer expects to play his best the first time out. But you can get your game into shape quicker by putting the following tips into practice.

Prepare for the New Season

I have a suspicion you've already begun the rites of spring. You've dug through the storage closet and hauled out the set of golf clubs. There's already a glint of sunshine in your eyes. The first bulbs are popping through the ground if you're in a northern climate. It's time to start thinking seriously of golf again.

If you're planning to use the same set of clubs again, the first thing I would check is their over-all condition to make sure they're playable again for another year. You might need a new set, or half a set, some new wedges or some new woods.

If the wood is just starting to crack, maybe shellac would help it. Put a coat of shellac on and buff it up. On the irons, see if the chrome is starting to chip or the grooves are gone. You must check the grooves to see if they're basically up to par with USGA standards. Without getting too technical, a groove can't be wider than 1/32-inch and the distance between grooves can't be greater than three times the width of a groove.

If you're going to stay with them, check the grips of the clubs. If you're a pretty good golfer, the grip will remain basically the same. This means the thumbs on the right and left hand hit the leather about the same place and have a tendency to wear. So leather may have to be checked and replaced.

Rubber has a tendency to wear a lot longer than leather. I personally use rubber and would advocate it for other people.

Check Yourself

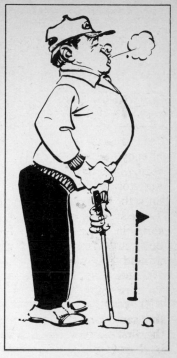

In getting ready for a new season, it's important for younger golfers to check if their own dimensions have changed since last year—if they've grown some, put on weight, if their hands have grown any or their fingers are longer. As they grow, their swing will change. They'll pick up a little more power. They might need a change in shafts, particularly in length.

On the subject of shafts, I might throw in a word about the magic new name, aluminum. I've had good reports on aluminum shafts. I don't mean to sound cocky, though, but I've had a tendency to stay away from anything new as long as I'm successful. I don't say a change wouldn't improve me, but I'm playing well enough now so that I don't mess with innovations. I have heard that the aluminum shaft will not be lasting, that there's going to be something better in a new stainless steel shaft in a few years.

While taking inventory, start at the bottom. How are your cleats? You can replace them at any pro shop if they're worn down. The shoes should be comfortable. I know some pros like Arnold Palmer would like to wear a new pair every day if it were feasible—that's how pliable golf footwear has become.

As for the rest of your outfit, it depends who your idol is. If you're a Frank Beard man or a Ben Hogan, old black and white is good. Or you can go real wild and have some kind of brown. But if you're down Doug Sanders' alley, you'll go for the new pastels.

The important thing is to have some ready equipment as rain gear. I keep an extra sweater in my bag, a hand warmer, a hat and, at times, a toboggan (or stocking) cap for bad weather. **It pays to be prepared.**

Get in Shape

I'd like to have started with Old Doublechins six months ago to get him shape for golf. You can do things over the winter that are very basic to staying in condition. It's as simple as setting up a net in your garage or basement to hit a few balls.

I do this at home in Louisville over the holidays. You can't always tell the results of the shots, but it keeps the same muscles active that you use on the course, keeps them loose all winter long.

Take a few basic exercises outside with the club. One is the old behind-the-arms bit. You'll know what I mean if you've ever seen Rocky Colavito in the on-deck circle at a baseball game, holding the bat behind his back and stretching to loosen himself.

If you're an avid practice tee golfer, the first 50 balls or so that you hit will rub some blisters on your hands. I can lay off two weeks and find that I rub blisters. The fellow who has laid off since last November is really going to be in trouble. The old hands are going to be soft, no matter if you wear gloves or what cautions you take.

I advise that you hit a few balls every day, maybe play nine holes, do some chipping and putting and get back in the swing of things.

Go Easy at the Start

In December last year, I didn't play a lick of golf. There was one 18-hole round in Louisville from Thanksgiving till Jan. 3. Then I went straight to Palm Springs, four days before the Bing Crosby Invitational. My muscles, because I play all year long and because of my age (28), don't become quite as tight. It doesn't take me long to swing back into shape.

All I have to do is watch my hands. I hit balls in the morning, played a few holes and hit balls in the afternoon. Four days, and I was starting to shape up.

Of course, my legs are in good condition and my wind, because of the walking. I do some situps and things like that but not nearly as much as I should.

I mentioned my routine to illustrate the gradual approach. Start the first day you're out playing golf with a wedge or a nine-iron. Something short. If you feel you should be hitting 110 yards with a nine-iron, try hitting it 90 yards with 50 or 60 balls to get the muscles stretched. **Don't hit too many balls the first day or two.** Hit 50 balls next with an eight-iron and forget it.

The sun's out and your appetite's whetted, but you'll rue the day you go out and hit 200 or 300 the first day.

Even I have to watch my step because my hands are tender. There's no set rule for work progression with your clubs. But if you start on a Monday, by the following Sunday you should be ready to attack the course.

Soggy Course

The golf course, now you're getting on it again, is going to be in the same shape as your game. Rusty, to be perfectly honest. In the spring, courses have a tendency to be soggy. Wet turf gives me more trouble than any other playing surface, and it's the same for the everyday player.

You have to make adjustments to it. **Play the wet ball a little farther forward. You have a tendency to pick the ball.**

So I take more club. I find I take one more club in spring than in summer in an effort to swing free and not overextend myself.

For instance, at the 17th hole at Pebble Beach this year, it looked like a four-iron shot. The pin was up in the corner and the wind was behind me, of all things.

I had on long underwear and sweaters and a rain suit and with a four-iron I was going to have to swing way too hard. It was cumbersome with all that equipment, and I didn't want to press the four-iron. So I took the three-iron and kind of cut it up in there with a smooth swing.

Of course, as pros, we change radically on the tour from the Crosby, where it's rainy, windy and very damp, and the air is heavy, to the desert, where it's dry and the air is very light and we pick up quite a bit of distance. I've played five or six years so it's easy for me to adjust.

To people who don't have a chance at all conditions, it's doubly important to play it safe this time of year.

Putting Practice

Putting is the one phase of golf where you can't overdo the practice bit, no matter what time of year it is. People laugh at guys who make the living room rug a practice green. But the fact it isn't grass doesn't matter. It's a good exercise.

The important thing is keeping the stroke smooth. You can watch the putter. You can change a few things. You can always keep your touch and get the feel of the hands working together.

When you get on actual

greens conditions, start with short putts. Gary Player gave me some of the strangest, most useful advice I ever received. We were at Greensboro one year, and he was standing there hitting 18-inch putts. He had 100 balls and he was popping those 18-inchers in, one after another.

"What are you practicing those for?" I asked. "Obviously, you never miss them."

"That's right," he said, "but I'll tell you what. The greatest thing for putting is confidence. And the greatest thing for confidence is watching that ball go in the hole. I'll stand here until my confidence is high. The subconscious is watching that ball go in the hole.

"You see these other blokes here go out and putt those 10- and 12-footers and miss about 75 per cent. How can you build your confidence with missed putts?"

It seemed ludicrous at the time, but the more I thought about it, the more I realized he was right. So start short with your putts and build your confidence early.

Concentration

One of the keys in starting early and progressing toward a successful season is to reconcile yourself to the fact your game will not be sharp at the beginning.

Even as a pro, I find my mind wanders from time to time early in the season.

It takes a little while to regain a competitive edge, which is a mental thing, and every golfer, at any level, has to have that little spur to get his game at its peak.

During the current campaign, I found at Tucson in late February that I was concentrating much better than anywhere else. It seems to correlate with your improvement in shotmaking. As you play better, and every shot counts, your ability to isolate yourself and just emphasize the shot at hand increases.

At Tucson, it happened because I was in contention (and eventually finished second in the tournament).

You'll be shooting higher than your handicap until you shape up. The person that comes out and presses and tries to force his game too quickly will jeopardize his chances for success later in the season.

Grooved Swing

When does it all fall into place? When do the parts of your golf swing start clicking smoothly so that you know you're at the top of your form?

Well, speaking personally, I can say that even after a couple of months on the tour I'm still way off. My swing is in a general groove. I haven't changed any. I haven't gotten any longer or shorter. You watch me in Cleveland this summer and you watch me in the Crosby next year, and it'll look like the same swing. It hasn't changed in appearance.

But there's a difference in the early going. The muscles are tighter. Even hitting balls you don't get completely loose. It's not mental. You're just not in shape. Maybe your fingers are fatter. It's a matter of co-ordination. You don't feel quite right, and you have to play into it.

There's no specific point at which you can suddenly hit one shot and say. "That was it. Everything fell into place there, and I know it'll be there tomorrow." You don't play badly and hope that work and practice catch up with you.

At this point, you may need some help. Even pros on the tour run into slump and have trouble analyzing what their problems are. You want to make sure your game is headed in the right direction. That's where someone like the club pro can fit into the scheme of your early game.

A quick checkup can prevent you from reacquiring old, bad habits.

Taking Inventory

The extent to which you should jump into formal lessons at the start of a new season depends on how far advanced a golfer is with his game.

I'd go out first and loosen up and take a personal inventory. If you've played at all, you should know your game.

The fellow who knew what he was doing wrong last summer and was working on it, and maybe had it halfway or all the way licked, should be able to pick up by himself.

I believe in self-reliance. I pretty much watch myself. I don't have to go for any help generally, but that's because I was fortunate in growing up that I became well-acquainted with my swing. Golf is an individual game. I'm a hooker, so I just watch my grip and my tempo. I can always tell when I go wrong. Incidentally, I'm a hooker by choice. That's the way my game is built.

You don't want too many people looking at you and advising you on your swing. It's like a baseball batter who has too many coaches. Say, he's had one bad season. Every joker who's batted .200 in the minors starts telling him what he's done wrong and confuses him even more.

So if you need a teacher, stick with one man. If you can remember what the pro told you last year, work on that before you attempt something new. There has to be a reason for a lesson. Don't just say to the pro. "What am I doing wrong?" Ask him, "Why am I doing this wrong?" And if he's familiar with your game, he can tell you instantly and get you started on the path to a good season.

Professional Help

When I caution against taking advice on your game too freely, I'm not equating golf at the professional level with that on the club level.

The man on the tour is a different kind of animal. It's his business. We also have a great feeling of camaraderie. We know each other's games through constant play and observation and can spot faults in each other's methods.

Sometimes, for instance, I need a little help with my alignment. This year my putting was giving me a problem. I felt like I was stroking it real good, but not getting results. I've been playing with Charlie Coody for the last five or six years and he's intimate with my game—as I am with his.

"You've played with me, Charlie," I said to him one day, "and you know how good a putter I am. Why am I not playing good?"

He said, "It looks pretty simple to me. You're aiming left and coming through and pushing the ball back on line. If your timing is perfect, it'll go in, but it's not something you can count on time after time. The best thing to do is get back around straight and work on the consistent stroke."

If you've watched me recently, I jump around more than usual before I get set over my putt, but that's because I'm aware of the alignment problem now and I've got it back around pretty good.

It's different getting advice from a Charlie Coody than the hacker in your foursome.

THE
STROKE

THE STROKE

☐How well you play depends, of course, on how well you swing. A sound, consistent swing can be developed by anyone willing to devote a small amount of time and thought.

The Swing

The golf swing is a blend of details, balanced and in orderly arrangement by instinct more often than by deliberation. Knowledge of the details involved eliminates, not creates, confusion when this know-how is applied in fitting the details into a dependable composite.

Experts have agreed that any golfer who attempts to consciously apply any more than one detail of what he knows about the swing during the fraction of a second required for a swing, is not in his right mind or won't be for long.

Two of the three factors involved in hitting the ball—the grip, the address and the swing—can be correctly executed while the player is standing at the ball. Only the swing—a three-part movement (backswing, downswing, follow-through)—is complicated.

Correctly done, it is one, smooth fluid action of the hands, arms and body. Words alone cannot describe it. It must be felt. Something about a sound, properly executed golf swing communicates itself immediately to the swinger. It is a sensation—he feels good all over. The feeling comes right up the shaft and into the player's hands and arms.

What the Grip Can Do

People think that once a golfer attains professional status, he acquires some kind of divine inspiration and his game automatically jells. **I have the same problems as an 80-shooter. And that's why I must keep reverting to fundamentals in analyzing my game.**

Start with the grip. My left hand gets much too strong at various times. I have to fight it continually. The left hand moves too far to the right on the club. I have to keep the thumb more on top, or to the left.

So I'm continually checking my grip, especially when I get into what I call my over-the-top hooking game.

All my life, until three years ago, I was a relatively weak guy who was never able to hit the ball far enough. That's how I developed a strong left-hand grip. It gives you a more powerful shot off the club, but it also comes off driving with a hook. Subconsciously, as a kid, I fell into this habit to get more distance off the tee.

Now a guy like Nicklaus, he never had to—he could afford to keep his hands on top—because he had the strength. He doesn't need a strong grip.

Jack is different in one respect though—he uses an interlocking grip, with the first finger of his left hand hooked around the little finger of his right. That's because he has small hands. Theoretically, I should also use an interlocking grip, because I have short, stubby fingers, too.

But, like 98 per cent of the pros on tour, I use the Vardon overlap and it's worked out fine. I make one concession. I use undersized grips on my clubs because they feel good.

35

Vary Stance

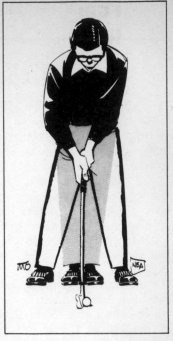

You've seen baseball players dig in at the plate, pawing dirt till they get comfortable. They're one up on golfers. They can use the same stance all the time. We've got to be more versatile.

The longer your shot in golf, the wider your stance becomes. On short shots, you keep it narrow for control.

There's also a divergence between the open and closed stance, according to the situation. I feel that the players on the tour now are leaning more to an open stance, in which the left foot is pulled away from the imaginary horizontal line paralleling the flight of the ball. That's because today's players are stronger and use better equipment.

A closed stance, with the left foot thrust inside the line of flight, provides more power. The players of another era, not as big and using hickory shafts instead of steel and aluminum, tended to the stronger stance.

So do a lot of baseball power hitters. Look at the way Stan Musial used to stand with his knee practically tucked up to his belt. He was actually turned around with a basically closed stance. Among today's players, Elston Howard is the most graphic example.

On the other hand, with the whipped bats and strong wrist action, guys like Willie Mays and Roberto Clemente can get by with their feet in the bucket, an open stance.

Golfers will vary their stance between open and closed to suit the occasion. They use the open stance for a softer shot that's going from left to right, or a fade. The hook is obviously from a closed stance. The longer power shots are from a closed stance, though many players have opened it up for more control.

Tempo Key to Backswing

The key to a backswing, the starting point for all golf shots, is correct tempo. Keep it slow and smooth and complete. Don't rush into your downswing.

There is, however, no uniformity to the length of the backswing. It varies with the height of the player and the tempo of his swing. Arnold Palmer has a short backswing because he has a very fast hitting stroke. Can you imagine him looping the club around his neck until it's almost down to his belt—like the long old Bobby Jones swing—with the speed he musters? He would never have anywhere near the necessary control of his clubhead.

For contrast, you have Sam Snead, with the slow, smooth, methodical swing. He can take the club back as far as he wants.

I'm more geared, personally, to the Snead school. I work on tempo. The slower the tempo, the more I can take the club back. I guess I approach 180 degrees with the shaft of the club parallel to the ground at the top of the backswing.

In my case, it used to be shorter. I've consciously made an effort to lengthen it because, as you get older, the muscles begin to tighten and restrict you.

That's what's happening to Doug Sanders. He's got that notorious half backswing, about 90 degrees to the ground. I feel he's not playing like he should this spring because his muscles have begun to tighten.

Yours will, too. I don't care how much conditioning you do. If you've started out with a long swing, you have that much more leeway as it starts to shorten up. That doesn't mean you have to be a Don January who brings the club back more than 180 degrees. Technically, he's overswinging. But that's Don. It works for him, and he's a champion. He'd change quickly enough if it didn't work.

37

Impact and Downswing

To review briefly, there are three basic parts to the striking of a golf ball—backswing, downswing and follow-through. After you've reached the top of your backswing, somehow you've got to get the club down and through the ball—slowly, smoothly, very firmly. **I personally advocate the use of the left side of your body—that is, uncoiling and initiating the swing with the left side in a lateral rotating motion.** This automatically drops the hands into the hitting area.

You don't start the downswing with the hands.

On theory, you should take the club straight back and then bring it straight through on the downswing. Obviously, this is almost impossible because of the way we're built. Our arms want to swing around—more horizontally than they do vertically. Put a man on a revolving pedestal and let the arms hang loosely, then spin the pedestal and his arms will swing out in a horizontal motion, never in a vertical golfing type of swing.

Now they talk about a grooved swing, the club in the same arc going back and coming down. Well, a fellow like Gay Brewer has a loop at the top of his swing. He never gets back in the same groove because the arc he started with is not where he wants to get back. He starts back to the outside and goes to the inside.

Gay has unusual club control. Most golfers are better off starting back on the inside and returning outside.

Follow Through

You've seen Arnold Palmer and Gary Player and other brilliant golfers on television, or maybe at their elbows in person, finishing a golf swing and looking is if they want to emulate the Leaning Tower of Pisa.

They're contorted in many different ways, none of them the smooth, effortless, flowing follow-through you visualize in textbook golf. Actually, they've expended so much energy in their swing and are so engrossed in the results that they couldn't care less what the finishing stance is.

And for efficiency it doesn't really matter. The follow-through has absolutely no importance in the swing itself, except as a check. If you could stop the club a foot on the other side of the ball, without affecting the force of impact, the ball would still go where it was directed.

The follow-through has no utility except as a way of checking your swing. It helps tell you if what has preceded the follow-through is correct.

The ideal to strive for is a high, extended follow-through, indicating that your arms haven't collapsed midway through the swing. You don't want to wind up with your arms wrapped around your neck.

Therefore, the hands, the arms and the club itself should be fully extended at the end of the swing, with the terminal point high and on the left side. You don't want to stay on the right side because in the course of your swing, your weight has shifted to the left side.

THE
IRONS

THE IRONS

☐A player who has mastered the irons is well on the way to being a really fine golfer. The iron shot is correctly executed by striking the ball on the downswing, producing the backspin necessary to get the ball close to the flagstick.

Irons In General

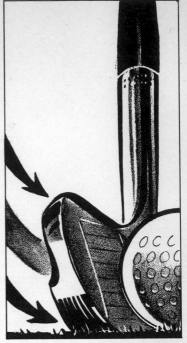

Because there are two kinds of golf clubs, woods and irons, there are also two kinds of swings required, as well as two different outlooks in what you can expect from e a c h club.

Irons in general are used for control and are never used for power or distance.

This is an elementary idea, but must be clearly understood before any success can be expected with your irons.

The biggest reason for a poor iron shot is overswinging or trying for too much distance. The iron is a delicate tool—even the long iron. They are used to zero in on the flag stick, and accuracy is all that matters.

An iron shot is struck with a descending blow, as opposed to woods, which are hit on the upswing.

This basic difference in the swings is how the two clubs differ in their results.

Because the woods are hit on the upswing, there is nothing but overspin imparted—hence the long distance that results, but sometimes with loss of control.

However, because the irons are hit on the downswing, the ball gets considerable backspin, the key to consistent control. This difference in swings and technique must be kept in mind at all times.

The thing to remember about good iron play is never under any circumstance to exert yourself with an iron.

Always take enough club and swing within yourself. The primary end of an iron shot is control and accuracy to the pin—leave the power and distance to your woods.

Maintain backspin with your iron shot and you will maintain control.

Playing the Short Irons

The short irons are the real "moneymakers" in your bag. They put the ball close for a one-putt birdie. These irons usually include the seven-to-nine irons and your pitching wedge.

Results with these clubs are generally much better for two reasons — the shafts are shorter and the loft on the faces is greater.

These two factors combine for pin-point accuracy if the clubs are used properly.

The mechanics for the short irons are very simple, but important to the success of the shot.

The first and most important thing to remember about good short iron play is the positioning of the ball at address. Because the shafts are shorter, the ball must be placed farther back in the stance than normal.

Another way to state this is that the ball must be positioned closer to the right foot than normal. This adjustment allows for the shorter radius in the short iron swing and allows you to strike the ball a descending blow—which of course imparts the important backspin.

Take it to the other extreme. For example, if the ball were placed too far forward, you could never get to the ball because the shaft would be too short to reach the ball position. **You would have to lean forward to reach the ball which, of course, would prove disastrous.**

Again, because the short irons are shorter-shafted clubs and are not required to be hit too far, a shorter backswing may be employed to maintain control. This is not a must but can be employed as the individual sees fit.

Always swing within yourself and your short irons will pay handsome dividends.

Middle Irons

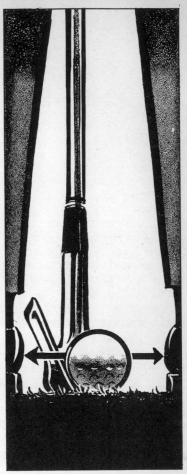

The middle irons are probably the most important irons in the bag because the average golfer will hit more middle-iron shots than all of the rest combined.

They differ from the short irons in that they have longer shafts and considerably less loft. However, the swing itself does not change considerably.

Remember, the key with any iron club is to try only for control, not power.

A couple of minor changes s h o u l d be made with your middle iron play. These irons usually include the four, five, and six irons—but can vary according to how many clubs and what kind the golfer carries.

The first adjustment is to play these irons somewhere near the middle of your stance. Because of their longer shafts, they will naturally be played farther forward than the short irons, but not as far forward as the long irons.

Secondly, the swing must be lengthened more than the short-iron swing to enable you to handle "a little more club." This adjustment is not mandatory if the individual thinks he is strong enough to swing each iron with the same swing.

But if your shots are weak and going to the right, then lengthening your swing can correct this.

48

Long Irons

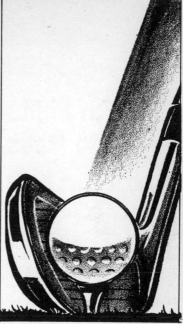

The long irons are often the most difficult clubs for the everyday golfer, and even the pros, to handle and maneuver properly.

This results from the fact that the shafts are much longer than any other iron club and that the loft is practically nil in relation to the other clubs.

I might deviate here for one thought that differs radically from what I have been stressing about iron play. The long irons will include the one, two and three irons. It sometimes is possible to try for a little power and distance with these clubs, but they are the only irons you should ever try it with, and then only under certain conditions.

It is a good idea to use these clubs off the tee in very tight situations and on short, narrow holes where distance is not a factor. The long irons can become invaluable "driving clubs" because of the confidence they instill.

But you should again maintain our basic approach to irons —swing within yourself and only for control and accuracy to the pins.

That's where you can get in trouble with your long irons. Because they are longer, with less loft than is ordinarily comfortable, there is a tendency to force or overshoot these clubs and try to "help" them into the air.

This problem can be eliminated very easily.

First, always keep your swing smooth and fluid as with the short irons. Try to imagine yourself swinging a nine iron when you are actually swinging a two iron and the results will be amazing.

Don't worry about getting these clubs airborne. They were not meant to be hit as high as the other irons. Let the club do all of the work.

Fat Shots With Irons

A fat or heavy or deep — whatever you want to call it—iron shot is the No. 1 nemesis of the average golfer. And the person to blame for this is your pro.

However, the blame lies only indirectly—that is, if he doesn't correct you when your trouble begins.

A fat shot stems directly from your early teaching to hit down on the ball with an iron.

Here your problems begin. Many players think that the golf swing is one piece—hit down on the ball and forget the rest—that hitting down will take care of everything. They forget that the follow-through is equally important.

So, in an effort to strike a descending blow, they chop down viciously into the ground and forget the rest.

The result is all ground and dirt and no ball.

The actual swing is a descending blow, but this must be accompanied by the rest of the swing—authority in the hitting area and a complete follow-through.

For the more advanced player, fat shots often result from moving off or away from the ball. On the backswing, if the head and shoulders move away or sway from the ball, then your entire arc is moved from its original framework and the impact area for the club is away from the ball.

Remember to use an entire swing—not half a swing. Try to remain over the ball throughout the swing and to "finish high."

Overcoming Bad Lies

Bad lies serve up headaches for pros and duffers alike. They are inevitable and must be accepted as part of the game.

If a person can realize that he gets many more good lies than bad, reconcile himself to this fact, and then execute this shot with a calm attitude, he will conquer the trauma of bad lies.

Bad lies can be classified into hilly, heavy or deep, plus those unfortunate ones that come to rest in divots and holes.

The hilly lies seem to offer the biggest problem but can be easily overcome with some basic knowledge of these situations.

On a downhill lie, the key is to remember that the ball will be harder to get airborne. Therefore, you must take a more lofted club than usual and play the ball farther back in your stance.

The reverse is true for uphill lies. Because the ball is so easily airborne it will not carry as far as desired, so you must take a less lofted club than would ordinarily be required and play the ball farther forward.

Heavy or deep lies cause great consternation because the ball has a tendency to fly farther than normal and is much harder to control because of the lack of backspin.

When you catch one of these lies, select less club than would ordinarily be needed and swing as smoothly as possible. You should also make an effort to shoot only for the middle of the green, since control is usually lost.

The "divot" lies are the most unfortunate. Take a lofted iron and make the best of this situation as possible.

The Wedge Is Valuable

In the last 30 years, the wedge has become the most valuable club in a player's bag. It is the utility club, the vital stroke saver that can compensate for a poor shot or put an approach close for a birdie.

I have often wondered what the great players of a few years back could have scored if they'd had access to a wedge.

Today's player often forgets what an asset he has in his bag. In fact, he shies away from the wedge as he would a snake or some childhood bugaboo. I hear all kinds of excuses for not using a wedge, when actually it is the easiest of all clubs to use successfully.

The key to great wedge players is practice to instill confidence, the elemental factor in any consistent success.

The wedge is used to escape trouble, such as bunkers and traps, and short recovery shots around the green. I have also found the wedge valuable as an approach club.

There are two kinds of wedge—the pitching wedge and the exploder or sand wedge.

I would recommend the pitching wedge for intermediate approaches. When you have a shot that is obviously too short for a nine iron, then the wedge is an invaluable tool.

This club should be used and mastered because it can save you many strokes.

It is actually a very easy club to use because of its mechanical construction.

The distinguishing characteristic of the wedge is a large flange on the bottom and back of the club. This flange insures against digging in behind the ball.

Once you have convinced yourself of this, the wedge, with some practice, can become your most trusted friend.

Hooks And Pulls

When the ball travels on a line to the left of your target, it can be one of two types of errors—a hook or an actual pull. These two miscues are very different with an iron than they are with a wood.

A hook with an iron comes from an inside-out swing with the hands and wrists revolving very quickly around the ball.

This type of action starts the ball out to the right but sends it bending on a line to the left very rapidly—with no control.

A slight hook that can be controlled is a desirable thing. In fact, it is much easier to control this type of shot than to attempt a straight shot.

To correct a hook with an iron, you must make an attempt to take the club back a bit straighter rather than inside. Then the hands must follow through in a straight line to the pin.

I find that I have great success when I use one small gimmick. I try to make my divot itself one straight line to the target. If this can be accomplished, the ball will also follow the same line.

The pull with an iron is an entirely different error. This shot does not bend at all to the left. It starts immediately to the left and travels a straight line to its undesired destination.

The pull results when the clubface comes from the outside across the ball with a square face.

This outside-across action obviously starts the ball to the left and can be overcome basically the same way the hook is corrected. Use the same gimmick I mentioned before.

Slices And Pushes

A slice or push with an iron is a chronic ailment of the everyday golfer. They are definitely very common to the beginner because his hands and wrists have not developed golf-wise.

Slices and pushes are exactly opposite in execution to the hooks and pulls. However, correcting slices and pushes is always much more difficult because we don't stand behind a golf ball when we hit it.

The slice is caused when the club strikes the ball from outside in with a cutting motion and very weak or slow hand action.

This is probably the hardest error in golf to correct, because it comes from trying to hook the ball improperly. In an effort to hook the ball, a slicer comes across the ball trying to force the ball to the left but actually all that happens is cutting the ball farther to the right.

In effect, the slice must be corrected by learning to hook.

This sounds a bit confusing but, believe me, it's the only way to handle a chronic slice. Get the club back a bit on the inside and hit out on the ball—not across it.

When I find myself slicing, I try to hit the ball to "right field." In other words, instead of coming across the ball to the left and slicing, I try to hit inside-out.

But watch out: Don't take this advice to the extreme, because this action can cause a push if the inside-out move becomes too extreme. You must only take the club a small bit to the inside and actually go through on a straight line.

It should only be exaggerated when your slice seems hopeless. When a push to the right begins to develop, less drastic action should be employed.

Picking the Right Iron

There is more to picking the right iron than estimating the correct distance to the hole and taking the corresponding iron. Many more factors go into the proper selection.

The first factor is the wind. There are different types of wind shots I'll discuss later.

But in selecting the iron, always check to see if there is wind and in which direction it's blowing.

If it is behind you, less club will be required; and if it is into you, more club is needed.

The second thing to be considered is the way the greens are holding the shots. For instance, say you have 150 yards to the pin, which ordinarily would require a seven iron. But the greens have been very hard and not taking the spin at all. Then you would want to land short of the hole instead of carrying all the way in.

Therefore, you would select an eight iron and land some 10 to 15 yards short of the hole and roll in the rest of the way.

The third factor is general weather conditions. In winter, the air is colder and heavier and thus the ball will not carry as far as usual and a longer club must be selected.

The opposite, of course, will hold true in the summer.

Whenever you play in the desert, the air is much lighter and again the ball will carry much farther, and less club must be selected than ordinarily.

The key to weather is just good common sense. Take inventory of the conditions in which you are playing and simply make a logical deduction as to what will happen to the ball, and select your club accordingly.

Understanding Backspin

Backspin is one of the most misunderstood terms in golf. Many golfers think that backspin just comes naturally, and some think they will never see backspin of any sort.

It can be very difficult to impart to the ball, and other times you can't avoid it. If used properly, it can save many strokes.

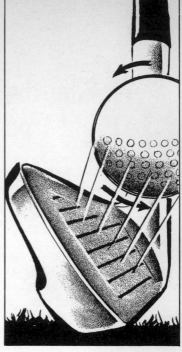

Generally speaking, backspin is imparted by striking straight down as if you were trying to chop off the rear half of the ball. However, the average golfer feels that he must alter his swing to get backspin and louses up his shot.

So another way of expressing the same idea is to try and pinch the ball between the club face and the ground.

The swinging action is not what actually spins the ball. The grooves in the club do it.

Once an individual reassures himself that the grooves on the club will do all of the work, his backspin problems are eliminated. Backspin is often lost by trying to do the work yourself.

Another type of spin closely related to backspin, and which will actually do the job as well, is a side-spin that comes from laying your club face wide open and cutting the ball.

This shot is used when you have to clear some trouble and don't have much green to work with. You lay your wedge wide open or flat and cut right-angles to the ball.

This sends the ball in a very high trajectory with side-spin as if the ball were slicing.

When this ball strikes the green it has a tendency to land softly and spin a bit to the right—not forward.

Let your club do the work and backspin will come naturally, and will also become another club in your bag.

High Fade For Control

Because golfers eventually get around to hooking, and I might add without much success, there has been a need for some type of shot that is dependable and can be called upon in the clutch.

A hook is very hard to control because it resembles a driving shot with a generally much lower trajectory.

The hook is hard to hold on a green, and the ball often runs into trouble.

In the past two years, I have developed a shot that has given me a great deal of control when the pressure is on. It is really not difficult to execute and can be used after only a short practice session.

It is what I call a high fade. Actually, it is more high than fade, but the result is the same — a shot that comes down dead on the green and which will stay on the green and out of the sand traps and high grass.

The mechanics are very simple — not much different than would be employed for a straight shot.

The left hand is moved slightly to the left in the grip, which puts the left thumb more on top of the shaft. This keeps the hands from rolling over.

I open my stance a bit in relation to the pin which in turn opens the entire body as for a cut shot.

The last thing to remember is to take the club back slightly on the outside and to return with the face slightly open. This gives the ball a higher trajectory with a small fade.

When this ball hits the green, it will stay on and not run for trouble. It becomes a very dependable shot and one you will readily use in tight situations.

Irons in The Wind

The most difficult situation the golfer faces is trying to play a proper iron shot when the wind is blowing. The wind can play havoc with straying shots, but when used properly, the wind can also become an asset.

The real key to playing in the wind is never to exert yourself or overswing.

Always take plenty of club and let the wind help you. Once you begin pressuring and overswinging, you make errors which are compounded in a strong wind.

Into the wind, you take more club than normal and play the ball back in your stance more than usual. This gives you a lower flight into the wind and more important, gives you plenty of club to reach the pin without pressing to get home.

With the wind, you take less club than normal and again play the ball back in your stance.

Contrary to most beliefs, you actually want the ball low with the wind so that it won't be carried too far.

The most difficult winds to play are cross winds.

However, the right shot played **into** these winds, not with them, can result in some wonderful approaches.

Too often, today's player tries to fade with a left to right wind and hook with a right to left wind. But this takes all spin off the ball and drives it onto and off the green.

You should hook into a slicing wind and fade into a hooking wind.

When this is done properly, the effect is a dead ball that drops onto the green with no action at all.

Checkpoints For Irons

The first and last thing to remember about good iron play is that irons were made for control and accuracy — not for power and distance.

If this single idea can be ingrained into an individual, his iron play will improve immediately.

Never exert or overextend your iron game. Always take plenty of club and swing within yourself—good results will follow.

As for mechanics, remember the three dimensions of irons—the short, middle and long irons. Always play your short iron toward your right foot and take a shorter, smoother swing. The middle irons are played in the center of your stance and a little longer swing is used.

The long irons are played much farther forward and a much longer and stronger swing is desired.

However, all irons should be swung approximately the same—the two iron with the same rhythm and tempo as the nine iron. Never overswing or press your long irons—let the clubs do all of the work.

Remember that a ball that is higher and fading slightly will always hold a green better than a ball that hits the green hooking. Always keep the ball under control with a fade and you won't have much bunker trouble.

In the wind, it becomes increasingly important not to press or overswing. Let the wind help instead of hurt your shot.

Take your time in selecting the proper club and then let this club do the work for you.

THE
WOODS

THE WOODS

☐The wooden clubs are used for long-distance shots and are crucial for good scores on the long par fives. The ball is ideally hit on the upswing, producing as much overspin or roll as possible.

Woods In General

The wood club is the power club in your bag. It is the club with which you obtain your greatest distance. However, therein lies the cause for the greatest percentage of troubles with wood shots.

We will go into these problems later one by one. Let's say for now that although the wood will give you more power and distance than your iron clubs, any conscious attempt to gain more power than is 'built into the wood" will only result in trouble.

Contrary to the irons, the woods are played much farther forward in your stance and are hit with an ascending blow during the swing.

The wood has a much longer shaft than an iron, thus resulting in the forward positioning of the ball. And, of course, this in itself will require an ascending or upward arc at impact. You never attempt to put any backspin on a wood shot. These shots were made for greater distance and not pinpoint accuracy.

I wouldn't want to say that accuracy is not of primary importance with wood shots.

However, where the target with an iron is a 4½-inch cup, the landing area for a wood is generally a big fairway or somewhere on the green.

The key to wood shots is good positioning and a free and easy swing with very little effort. The mass of the head and the increased length of the shaft will do all of the work for you.

How to Use The Driver

The driver is the "big gun" of your wood clubs. It is used for the greatest distance you need. You should be able to get all the distance you need with a driver. However, remember to let the driver do all of the work. It is engineered to do the work itself—any help you try to administer yourself, like swinging harder or faster, will result in very poor drives.

For the driver, the ball is usually positioned farther forward (in relation to your stance) than for all the other woods because of its long shaft and because it is used with a tee. This position will enable you to get in behind and under your drives and get the ball into the air. You can also gain that extra overspin from this position.

Of all the clubs in the bag, I suppose the driver is mistreated the most. Everyone tries to hit it too hard or swing too fast or tries some other homemade method for extra distance. Actually, for best results the driver should be handled exactly as you would a short iron.

It is amazing how far and straight you can hit a drive with a nice slow, smooth swing.

When I get into trouble with my driver and can't seem to get it worked out, I try one thing that has worked for me quite a time now.

I go to a driving range and pick out some short distance marker, such as 100 or 150 yards. I then try to hit my driver just this distance with a full swing.

In an effort to do this, I slow everything down because distance is not a factor. As a result, my timing, accuracy and distance seem to return almost immediately.

Fairway Woods

The fairway woods are the "pin pointers" of the wood clubs. Often you use them for distance on long par-5 holes or for control off the tees. However, the majority of the time the fairway woods are used for accuracy in approaching the greens.

For this reason, it is very important that accuracy be kept uppermost in your mind when swinging your "three" and "four" woods.

These clubs should have the ball positioned farther back in your stance than the driver because the shafts are shorter and because the fairway wood shot quite often resembles an iron shot.

Because the fairway wood is often used from bad lies, you may have to use a descending blow to get the ball airborne. Playing this wood back farther in your stance will facilitate this action.

The primary trouble the average golfer has with fairway woods is getting the ball up in the air. This will be handled later on but positioning is one of the keys. Playing the ball too far forward or too far back can cause this problem.

The thing to remember about your fairway woods is that they are used for long distance accuracy. Never try to get more from the shot than you need and just let the club do all of the work.

Don't try to help the ball into the air—let the loft on the club face take care of this.

Swing slow and smooth and let the club do all of the work and your results will improve tomorrow.

Topping The Woods

Without a doubt, the biggest problem that the average golfer has with his woods is topping them. The reason for this is basically a lack of mechanical knowledge which causes a lack of confidence in your wood clubs.

Topping the ball can be pinpointed almost 100 per cent to the false impression that the player must get the ball into the air himself, that the club cannot do this—the player must do it himself.

Therefore, he does everything he can to get the ball airborne except the right thing. He tries to play the ball too far forward, tries to scoop it up with a shovellike motion, etc. All that results from all of these attempts is a big top.

As I have said before, the clubs you possess were engineered long ago to do the job themselves. They don't need any help from you other than to use a good smooth golf swing.

They have plenty of loft to get the ball into the air—all you need do is swing the club properly. Don't try and help the ball up—have confidence in your clubs and let them do all of the work.

When you try to help the ball up, all you do is swing over the ball. Result: you top it.

Swing as though you were trying to hit a long straight smooth putt. You don't swing up on your putter—but through.

Well, the same idea holds true of your woods. Just give them a chance with the proper swing.

Hooking The Woods

Hooking with the woods is very similar to that with the irons. However, the results are far worse because of the extra power and distance.

Although the error is practically the same as in iron play, the correction is somewhat different because of the ascending blow of the woods and the different positioning of the ball in your stance.

A hook with a wood club is generally caused by rolling the wrists through the ball too fast or letting the right hand pass the left before impact.

Rolling the wrists to the left has to be done some time during the swing or you would break your hands.

However, when this is done too soon and too fast, it has a tendency to make the clubface do exactly the same thing, which in turn obviously will induce a hook.

You must keep the hands and wrists moving straight through the ball until AFTER the impact, then let them turn over. Any sooner than this will cause a vicious hook.

The other general cause of a hook is to position the ball too far forward in your stance.

If the ball is too far forward, then the hands have uncocked by the time they reach the ball. That is, the right hand has passed the left before it reaches the ball instead of after it passes the impact area.

Always position your ball so the hands can lead into the impact area with the wrists still cocked.

Once they have begun uncocking before reaching the hitting area, the club leads with the impact and the result is a hook.

Slicing
The Woods

For the golfer who has learned to get the ball airborne consistently, the most prevalent error is the slice.

The slice with the woods occurs exactly as the slice with the irons. Although the lengths of the shots differ, as do the positioning of the ball, the faults in the swing that cause the slice remain the same.

For quick review, a slice results from bringing the club from the outside in across the ball, which imparts a slice spin. The key is to get club back inside the line so that you can hit from inside out, keeping the right elbow tucked close to your side at all times on the downswing.

However, as with the irons, this problem often becomes more mental than physical. The golfer feels that he is going to slice, so he fights it by trying to pull the ball back to the left. All he does is emphasize his slice even more.

The best way to fight a slice is to convince yourself that you are going to hit from the inside out, no matter how helpless it feels. You have to have the feeling that you are hitting out to right field.

Once you have conquered the basic knowledge of the whys and wherefores of a slice and how it must be corrected mechanically, then the only problem that remains is conquering your own mind.

That, unfortunately, is a personal battle. No pro in the world can help you with mind-over-matter. It just takes a little self-discipline.

Skying The Woods

Another headache that the golfer must encounter is "skying" or popping up the driver, or any wood shot for that matter. But the driver is more common because of its teed-up position.

However, contrary to popular belief, teeing the ball high has absolutely nothing to do with popping it up. The error lies elsewhere.

Tempo, or the loss of tempo, is the culprit in this case. Generally, when you swing too hard and fast, something goes wrong. Sometimes it is a hook; sometimes a slice or top—or as in the present case, the pop-up.

It's like driving a nail into a board. What would happen if you took the hammer back and forth in a flash as fast and as hard as you could? I'd hate to see the hand that held the nail.

Well, the same is true for a golf swing—swing hard and fast and the results will be far from satisfactory. Make every move deliberate and with precision, and you begin to eliminate your errors.

Actually with a pop-up, you have probably swung so fast that the hands have gone into the impact area so far ahead of the body that the clubhead is way out in front, and you have caught the ball on the biggest part of the upswing. There is no drive or body in the flight of the ball— the pop-up results.

Slow your swing down, and deliberately hit that nail right in the back with precision and smoothness.

Getting Extra Distance

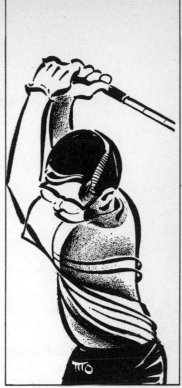

There are several different ways of obtaining extra distance with the driver.

However, let me caution you against trying for anything but accuracy until your swing is well-grooved and you have complete control of every facet of it.

If you don't then any attempt to gain more length will only throw off everything else, and you will have all the basic work to redo.

The best way to increase your distance is to increase the length of your backswing. The length of a drive is in direct proportion to the amount of clubhead speed with which you strike the ball. The speed in turn is itself increased by a longer, slower backswing. The longer and slower the swing, the more time and distance there will be for building up clubhead speed.

But remember this change will make the swing just that much harder to control. Until this control returns, your distance will increase, but your accuracy will suffer.

The other way I recommend for obtaining extra distance off the tee is using the bottom part of your body in the swing more than usual.

This actually means to generate or begin your swing with your legs. Imagine your swing as a spring that has coiled up. This spring is released at the bottom and whips the rest of the spring into action.

This could also be true of your swing if you can learn to generate the upper part of your torso with your legs. You'll get more clubhead speed with the entire body taking part, instead of only the arms and hands.

Woods That Cut Strokes

The rules of golf allow a player to use only 14 clubs at one time, so he has no room for any extra or auxiliary clubs.

However, many players carry certain clubs they cannot use well and which only take up room in the bag.

If these dead clubs could be eliminated and replaced with some stroke-savers, scores could really be helped and with no changes in the swing.

I'd like to offer two recommendations concerning the driver and the two-iron.

These two clubs give the average player the most trouble, and he usually winds up making some kind of substitution with a club that already is in his bag. I would advise trying a 1½-wood or even a brassie for the driver and replacing the two-iron with a five-wood.

I honestly don't believe that you lose any distance with this smaller driver, and it is certainly easier to use than the big regulation driver. The reason I am so sure of this is that I use a small-headed 1½-wood myself. I never could use or control a big regulation driver, and since I have changed to the smaller one, I have actually increased my distance because of my strengthened confidence. My control has become a routine thing.

The five-wood substitution is really great for those golfers who are deathly afraid of their long irons. A wood is easier to hit and to get the ball up in the air. It instills confidence almost immediately.

Give this club a real tryout and see if your long iron problems don't begin to disappear.

Uphill And Downhill

Some of the most serious problems with wood shots arise from bad lies. The worst are hanging lies. These lies include uphill, downhill, and sidehill positions that completely eliminate any hope of a normally level stance. However, these lies pose no real serious threats if the player knows what to expect and how to cope with such situations.

The real key to these particular lies is to adjust your stance and balance so that your shoulders and line of sight coincide with the actual plane of the ground itself.

For an uphill lie, you must keep most of your weight on the right side. This has a tendency to keep you back somewhat and keeps you from leaning forward into the hill.

The object is to tilt your shoulders back so that they become parallel with the ground. When this is done you have actually come as close as possible to a level stance.

From an uphill lie, take more club than normal because the trajectory will be higher than normal and will not carry as far as desired.

The reverse is true for downhill lies. Try to keep most of your weight on the left side so that you won't lean to the right into the slope of the hill. Keep the shoulders parallel to the ground and try as best you can to obtain a stance level with the actual contour of the hill.

From this downhill lie, take less club than usual. Since the flight of the ball will be lower, you will need more loft than normal to get the ball airborne.

The thing to remember again is to keep your shoulders and stance parallel to the slope that you are on and swing as though you were on a level piece of ground.

Proper Teeing For the Ball

Too often I see a player tee up for a drive in any place he comes to first. There is no attention paid to the side of the tee which might be more advantageous to the type of shot that has to be executed.

Well, actually knowing how to tee the ball properly can give you much the best of the deal when you have to hook or fade a shot from the tee.

When you must play a hook or a draw from the tee, you should always tee up on the extreme left side of the teeing area.

This procedure will automatically aim you to the right side of the fairway so that you will have the entire fairway to hook back into.

If you have teed-up on the right side you would be aiming at the middle or the left side of the fairway, so your hook or draw would actually have very little room to maneuver in.

The reverse is true for a fade or slice. Tee the ball on the extreme right side of the tee box so that you will automatically be aligned on the left side. This will again offer the entire fairway as a target, since your fade or slice will start down the left side and work back into the fairway.

Of course, when you aren't sure what kind of shot you will hit or when you are attempting to hit a straight shot, then you should tee up in the middle of the teeing area.

Your initial aiming will be right down the middle.

This will give you a 50-50 chance if you make a mistake and don't hit the straight ball you had hoped for.

Give yourself a decent chance the next time you tee off.

The Club Does the Work

I have mentioned before, almost to the point of being repetitious, the idea of letting the club do all of the work. As far as I am concerned, this is the most important aspect of swinging at the ball properly. Any time you try to do the club's work or to add anything extra into the shot, your results will be unsuccessful.

After you have convinced yourself that you have good equipment and that it has been engineered and constructed properly to do the job it was made for, then you must begin working on a swing which will let the club do its job.

Such a swing is based primarily on rhythm and tempo alone and is completely devoid of any home-grown mechanisms to help the shot along. You must concentrate on swinging the club exactly the same every time under any circumstances.

Rhythm in a golf swing is much the same as in dancing —you just flow with whatever comes along—don't force yourself or your club.

When I am swinging my best I always have the feeling that I have too much club for a particular shot. In this way, I never overexert a swing. I am always trying to hold back and swing smoothly. I only get into trouble when I have the feeling that I don't have enough club and try to swing too hard and get more out of a shot than I can.

So the tip I pass along in your attempt to develop rhythm and the proper tempo is never to overswing or exert yourself.

Always take a little more club and get the feeling that you have the club and your swing under complete control. Let the club do all of the work, and you take a rest!

Driving
In the Wind

The average player is most likely to lose his composure and begin to press and swing hard under windy condition.

This is actually the time when he must call upon his smoothest, most rhythmical swing. When a golf shot is struck properly, the wind will bother the flight very little; it is only when a shot is muffed that the wind takes over and exaggerates the error.

Of course, hitting into the wind is the most difficult driving situation. It's tough only because the player forces the shot and tries to overpower the wind itself. The wind has very little effect on the ball; the player is the cause of shortness. In his effort to drive harder into the wind, he hits the shot poorly. It wouldn't go anywhere, wind or not.

The key to driving into the wind successfully is to swing smoothly and hit the ball solidly every time; solid contact will always insure good results.

Driving with the wind, strangely enough, poses parallel problems, for different reasons. Downwind driving gives a player a false sense of security. He feels that he can really give it a big swing downwind and get all kinds of extra distance.

The result is the same: in his effort to put a big swing on the ball, he hits the ball badly and it doesn't go anywhere after all.

Again the key to good driving downwind as well as into the wind, is to swing smoothly and contact the ball solidly time after time.

Different Drives

After you have developed your game to the point that you can score fairly well, you will see that your bad holes can be attributed directly to bad drives. And this usually comes from the fact you don't know how to keep the ball in play after you are off the tee.

You cannot consistently hit the ball straight with the same type of drive every time. You must have a variety of drives that you can call upon under different circumstances. Remember wind conditions vary, the width of fairways can change, and different types of holes call for different drives.

The drive that I have found to be most successful in keeping the ball in play is what I call a "squibbler." It resembles a low fade and is not a very pretty shot. However, it is very effective and keeps the ball in play.

I play the ball back in my stance somewhat and open the stance up a few degrees. I don't actually use a full swing but more of a punch-type swing employing a slight cutting action. The shot comes off to the left a bit and fades back into the middle very nicely. I don't get much distance with this shot, but my control is almost flawless. I use it in very tight situations and when contact is of utmost importance. It takes a bit of practice, but it will work!

There are many different kind of drives that can be used under varying circumstances.

You must try several of these and find one that you can depend upon under pressure and in a tight situation.

Remember, keeping the ball in the fairway, even at a cost of distance, is the first step to lower scoring.

Wood Checkpoints

There are not many checkpoints for your woods, but each serves a purpose and is very important to the continued success of good woods.

The first check is the positioning of the ball at address. All woods are positioned farther forward in the stance than with irons. This is because of the longer shafts in wood clubs and the need for getting the ball airborne. Always keep the ball in a comfortable position, but as far forward as possible.

The essential key to good wood play is to let the club do all of the work. Don't help the club out with some homemade gimmick. The wood club is very capable of performing all the work itself. So just swing smoothly and with as little effort as possible and the club will do the rest.

When you are having trouble with uphill and downhill lies, you probably don't have your shoulders and line of sight parallel to the ground. Always keep your body and stance conforming to the slope as much as possible; then the club can be swung in a level plane to the hill.

For a little extra distance, try lengthening the backswing a bit, all the while remembering to not force it, but let the extra clubhead speed do the work.

Remember, the key to good wood shots is a combination of tempo and rhythm. Swing the club smoothly and without effort, and you'll be surprised at the excellent results you continue to get.

Driving For Accuracy

In golf, as in going down a flight of stairs, how you begin or take the first step determines how you arrive at your destination.

Of course, the first step in planning your golf game is proper driving. And the one and only thing ever to be conscious of in driving strategy is to keep the ball on the fairway. You must stay on the fairway at any cost.

Loss of distance and how the shot may look are secondary. I find that the biggest asset in consistent driving is to eliminate the straight ball! When a player aims down the middle and tries to hit a straight ball, knowing that he either hooks or slices most every shot, he is giving himself only half of the fairway to shoot at. However, if he deliberately makes the ball hook or fade and plans for this shot down the corresponding side of the fairway, he is actually getting full advantage of the entire target area.

For instance, if the player aims down the right edge of the fairway and hooks on purpose, he has the entire fairway to hook into, and vice versa for the fade. But if he aims down the middle and tries for a straight ball and it hooks, then he only has from the middle of the fairway to the left side, or 50 per cent of the target area.

Remember, if you miss the first step you will arrive at the bottom of the staircase, but I won't say in what condition. The same applies on the course. Keep the drive in the fairway and you will have a chance to arrive in par!

STROKE
SAVERS

STROKE SAVERS

☐This section is designed to do precisely what it says–Save Strokes. Here is help on getting out of the bunker in one shot: eliminating those three-putt greens; and much more.

Putting Psychology

I talked about the necessity of confidence in playing bunker shots. When it comes to the next, and perhaps most vital phase of golf, that confidence becomes the most important element.

No one can teach you how to putt. Successful putting is all in your head, with one physical proviso—you must be comfortable.

Styles vary. I grip the putter primarily in the fingers of the right hand, with the thumb on top of the shaft. My right hand does the major part of the stroking work, taking the club back and hitting it through the ball.

Like most of the pros, I use a reverse overlap, with the left forefinger over the fingers of the right hand, yet I never actually get the feeling that my left hand is doing anything.

My major adjustment in putting comes from the way I expect the putt to break after assessing the contours of the green and the grain of the grass. **For a straight putt, I'll use a square stance, the line of my feet parallel to the flight of the ball. For a putt that breaks to the right, I'll open up my stance, and for one that breaks to the left, I'll close it—** this footwork closely resembles the fading and hooking on normal shots, although not as exaggerated.

I'll add one word of caution. Keep your head still over the ball while in the act of putting. Moving it reflects your anxiety at seeing where the ball went, causing you to jerk your stroke. It also reflects a lack of confidence.

88

Downhill Putts

On long downhill putts, always be sure to stroke hard enough so that you are left with an uphill second putt. This of course does not apply to short downhill putts because you are trying to plunk the ball in the hole and not send it past.

Checking the green before hitting the long downhill putt is of primary importance. If the green goes from left to right, then the ball will break right. And vice versa from right to left. In other words, the ball breaks the way the green goes, like in ordinary putts.

Adjustments must be made for steep downhill putts, for simply small slopes and when putting from the side. It need hardly be said that the steeper the slope the swifter the ball will travel down.

I recall a recent tournament at Spyglass when Arnold Palmer had a steep 25-foot putt and misjudged the decline. He putted off the green, then had to come up and missed the hole.

The moral here is: be very cautious.

Reading The Greens

The two most important elements in reading the break on greens are checking the slope and the texture of grass.

Measuring the slope is elementary. The ball will break the way the green bends. That is, if slope goes from right to left, the ball will break left, and vice versa.

In grass texture, two points must be thoroughly considered. One is the grain. The second is the thinness or coarseness of the grass.

Grass, like slopes, bends in a certain direction. Again, the ball will break the way of the bend.

The texture of the grass varies around the country. In the North, the grass is more lush or coarse than in the South and West. Lush grass tends to make the ball roll slower. Sometimes, it's as sticky as glue, so you would give the putt more of a rap.

Also, Bermuda grass is coarser than the bent, or fine, grass.

I've misread millions of putts on Bermuda grass (and bent grass). But two that you may remember were on the 18th hole of the last round of the Tournament of Champions last year in Houston. I needed two putts to win. The first was from right to left. The second was left to right, and I sunk it.

Short Game

You've gotten back into the swing of your golf game. Now you're interested in the pleasure part—cutting down your score. Where do you start?

There's no contest here. It's got to be in the short game.

I feel that weekend golfers can keep their drivers and irons, their swinging clubs, moderately under control, at least to the point they can advance the ball. But their short game suffers miserably for the most part because they don't play enough for consistency.

Even in my own case, if I lay off for two or three days, much less two or three months in the winter, my short game starts to fall apart, the chipping or the putting.

So to save strokes, I definitely emphasize concentration on the short game in practice. Start from the 50-yard wedge shot on into your chips with the six- or seven-iron off the fringe of the green. Some people use a four-iron off the fringe.

Of course, there are decisions involving the use of a pitching wedge to lob the ball or running it up with an iron. I take pitching wedges more when the greens are hard and, consequently, fast. You get more loft and the ball doesn't hit the green with as much momentum. It's a bit contrary to my rule of getting the ball on the green and letting it run. But, as I noted, the conditions dictate the choice of club. I won't take a nine-iron when I can use a wedge if the greens are hard and the ball will run too much.

It's all in the feel. The short game separates the sensitive golfer from the hacker.

Getting Out of the Rough

When you have to wade through the rough to get to your ball, your thoughts must be centered on the type of lie you have.

Is it a good or bad lie? If it's a bad lie, then your strategy is very much like hitting from under the lip of a sand trap. **You use whatever club necessary to get out of there. If a wedge is needed to hack out, then use it.**

In a good lie, decide what club you would use from a similar position on the fairway. Then use one club less. For example, if you would use a 6-iron from the fairway on this shot, then use a 7 from the rough. That is because you are shooting with overspin from the rough, while you shoot with backspin from the fairway.

Generally, when you hit from the rough the ball has added momentum because of the overspin, and takes off like a misguided missile. This is what the tour golfers call "flying."

The overspin with the longer club makes up the 20 yards or so difference in distance. When you hit from the fairway, the ball stops almost immediately because of the backspin.

From a good lie, you can get to your objective from the rough the same way you can from a similar fairway position. You just take different routes.

Hazards of the Rain

Bad weather has sunk more golfers because of their attitude than because of the actual inclement conditions. Some golfers feel they must battle rain and cold rather than adjust to the conditions.

You just can't play "sunshine-type" golf when rain is splattering your face and drenching the ball and grass or when your body is goosepimply with cold. But many try.

The first rule for playing in the rain seems almost too obvious to mention: keep yourself and your equipment dry. If your clubs and grip are wet, you're finished.

Next, play the ball a little further forward, so it will have a tendency to "fly," as when playing out of the rough. Try to upswing or "pick" the ball off the grass. Don't hit down any more than you have to. This pick shot helps reduce slippage of the club face when meeting the wet ball.

When it rains, the air becomes denser than in better weather. This sometimes holds up the ball and cuts down on flying. Once you feel the ball is not flying, then go to more club.

The most important element in cold-weather playing is to keep warm. This may sound silly, but golfers often "underdress" because they feel that too many clothes will restrict their swing.

This may be true. But if you are cold, your swing won't be effective anyway. You won't have a free swing in any case, so make the best of the situation. Dress warm and swing within yourself.

From a mechanical standpoint, a good general rule is to use more club—because of the restricted swing—with a smoother and easier stroke.

Bunker Play

The one shot in golf that looks as if it should paralyze a golfer actually can be turned to his advantage. A sand or bunker shot shouldn't scare if you obey a few basic tenets.

First, of course, you plant yourself firmly. You've seen pros take the trouble to dig their shoes solidly as possible into the sand. Keep your basic grip. The sand wedge is an integral part of your equipment, a club to be swung with the same pattern as any other in the bag. Like the others, it's manufactured for a specific purpose.

The one variation from the norm is that instead of making direct contact with the ball, you take a minimal amount of sand with the swing. You also don't get a chance to address the ball in the sand because that would cost you a stroke penalty. With an open club face, you prepare yourself mentally to hit near the ball. **The trick here is to concentrate on a spot behind the ball where you expect to make contact.**

Then hit with confidence, in a normal arc, allowing the club to follow through. How hard you swing depends on the density of the sand and how deeply the ball is buried. The only sure gauge for this is an instinctive feel that comes with practice. That practice builds confidence, and confidence is the real key to good bunker play. Any pro worth his salt has it and, therefore, isn't harassed by the thought of playing out of sand. It's no tougher than a short chip from the fringe.

Lips of Traps

Greed is often the downfall of golfers confronted with a shot under the lip of a trap. They expect to get good loft as well as good distance to the green.

One just can't expect too much from such a position. The first—and possibly only—concern is to get out of there. Therefore, use any club that will serve that purpose. Use enough club to loft past the lip.

Worry about distance after getting over the lip is assured.

Once, though, I broke my own rule on this. It was on the 17th hole of the Master's a few years ago. I was trying to get in contention and was faced with a shot from the lip of a trap.

I decided to gamble because I felt I had nothing to lose and everything to gain.

I tried for loft and distance, but primarily distance. I swung, hit the lip and the ball rolled back. I lost the gamble.

But, it must be emphasized, that was a rare circumstance. And you saw how it paid off, anyway.

Imbedded In Sand Traps

Playing a ball imbedded in a sand trap is similar to most trouble shots: you can't expect too much. Get the best you can out of an unfortunate situation, then forget it.

Here, you play the ball back closer to your right foot than normal. **Keep the club face closed (or hooded) in this bunker shot.** This is in contrast to most bunker shots in which you keep the club face open.

When you're lined up, **swing down and through the ball, hitting about an inch behind the ball. It's a chopping swing.**

Keep in mind that you must allow for considerable run, since no backspin can be imparted.

Of course, it is a frustrating shot at best. The best antidote I can recommend is that you stay clear of traps altogether.

But that's like saying you shouldn't catch cold. And no one has yet found an adequate cure for either.

Freak Shots

I would never advocate the average golfer using freak shots because there is always the possibility of hitting yourself in the leg. Sometimes, though, there is no other way to save a stroke.

I have used three types of freak shots in tournament play. They have usually occurred when I have run up against a solid surface, like a fence or wall, that is not considered an obstruction.

A few times, I have had to hit the ball with a left-handed stroke.

A second freak shot I have employed is this: with my back to the objective (fairway or green), I spread my legs with the ball somewhat centered. I take the club and with a vertical, over-the-head stroke—as if chopping wood, or maybe like a football center snapping the ball—hit down.

Another time I have used a freak shot is when up against a tree. I have turned and assumed an orthodox stance, then hit the ball into the tree and hoped for a bank shot like in billiards.

Of course, that's not as bad as Arnold Palmer hitting the ball into the rotted stump of a tree at the 1963 U.S. Open in Brookline and having to hack the ball out from there.

A Ball
In Water

The key to playing a ball in water is this: don't attempt to hit any ball that is completely submerged. Take the penalty and get out. But if even one dot is sticking out, then you can hit it.

When the ball is partially out of the water, your club face should be closed and you should follow through. Though water is denser than sand, these two trouble shots are played similarly.

Going into water is a personal thing. I don't advocate any special means. I usually take off my shoes, roll up my pants and wade in. But I don't like to go barefoot in shale or coral bottom water like they have in California.

Most courses on the tour have mud or sand bottoms. Sometimes I have gone into water wearing shoes. I felt I could get better footing than going in barefoot. I don't worry about a $30 pair of shoes when $20,000 is at stake.

Luckily, I haven't had much trouble with water as a pro. I do recall a shot from the water when I played in the Texas state junior tournament several years ago. I hit into the creek. The ball was sitting on a rock, about one-fourth submerged. I used a full 6-iron and hit onto the green.

To sum up, if the ball is completely submerged, take the penalty. I wouldn't recommend using a snorkel for that shot.

98

Water Hazards

Water hazards should not, of course, be ignored. But neither should they prey on your mind.

When upon a water hazard, the first thing you do is look the other way. If it is right, look left to see what kind of trouble there is at that point. Then go for the lesser of the two evils.

You have to decide which is worse, the water or possibly going out of bounds in trees. If there is rough opposite the water, I usually take that route.

This may be a conservative way of playing, but it keeps me out of water.

The eighth hole at the Los Angeles Open has a canal to the left of the green and water coursing around to the right, just short of the green.

You can either hit it short or hook it over and to the left. I like to go left. I use plenty of club. I start right and then draw it in.

I have pretty fair luck that way. But, like all water hazards, it keeps you on your toes.

Poor Fairway Lies

"Fluffy" shots and divot shots are the two most common poor fairway lies.

"Fluff" shots usually occur when the grass hasn't been cut and the ball is nestled among the blades. Here, I use one less club than in ordinary circumstances because you are bound to get a "flyer." The ball will come shooting out. Since it will hit and run, you play shorter. So, if you would normally use a 6-iron, say, then go to your 7.

The situation is reversed in the fairway divot. Here, you take one more club and punch out and toward the hole.

It is similar to hitting from under a tree.

Fairway Grass

Three types of grass are commonly found on fairways and greens: Bermuda, bent and bluegrass (or water grass).

Bermuda grass is the softest of the three. It is invariably found in Florida and Texas. The ball sort of sits up on it. Shots on this type of grass have good spin and good stick.

Bent grass, however, is conducive to flying shots. It is finer than Bermuda. The ball will settle in the grass and, when hit, tends to jump and fly.

Bluegrass is usually found in the Midwest. It is just a bit coarser than bent. And the ball takes off just as it does on bent grass. Here, too, watch for flyers.

Course Management

The biggest trouble the average player gets into on the golf course comes from his own mental approach to the game. He faces a 500-yard par-five hole from the tee, and he starts puffing up his muscles to explode the ball halfway down the fairway. Instead, by overswinging, he shanks it or tops it or slices it out of bounds.

If your normal distance is 200 yards, why risk an extra shot or even strokes by trying for 250.

Play within yourself.

That goes for the shorter holes, too. Take a par-three 220-yard challenge, well-trapped. As pros, we're expected to be on the green in one. That's our business. But Mr. Average Player may not have the capacity to put a 200-yard tee shot in a little target area.

I see nothing wrong in using a shorter iron and putting the ball in good strategic position in front of the green. With a good pitch shot, you could still salvage par with one putt. At the very least, you should wind up with a neat bogey.

That may sound like ultraconservative advice, but it is meant constructively for a segment of golfers who are not addicted to shooting a round in the 70s. That takes in a sizeable group, I might add, or the relatively few of us who play golf for a living would be in trouble.

And trouble is what we're trying to avoid in golf.

Dealing with Obstructions

When entangled with ob-
structions, one normally either
shortens his swing or his grip
(that is, the length of the shaft
becomes shorter).

These cases necessitate
more club to make up the distance cut down by the shorter
swing or grip.

**In using a shorter swing,
a punch-type stroke is employed. With a shorter grip,
you swing full.** The results, in
both cases, should be the
same as when not involved
with obstructions.

At Indianapolis recently, I
was under and slightly in front of a tree. Under normal
conditions it would have been a 9-iron shot. However, I
used an 8 and took a three-quarter swing. The ball popped
out and onto the green.

Someone else might even have used a 7. But the club
selection is purely a matter of knowing your game. And
that comes with experience.

FINE
POINTS

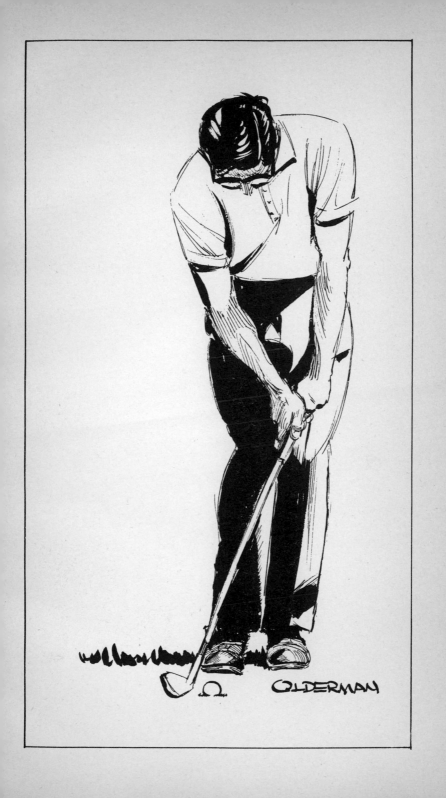

FINE POINTS

☐ Here are the extras—the fine points which while they won't make you play in the seventies can help you score better and enjoy the game more.

Percentage Approaching

There are more ways to approach a green than just blindly shooting for the flagstick. You must use certain precautions to insure some measure of consistency—what I call making the odds work in your favor.

When sizing up an approach, always note on which side of the green the pin is cut. This is important because the side away from the hole is the "fat," or safe, part of the green and the area which we will make our initial target.

If the pin is on the left side of the green, then you must start the ball to the right and draw it in across the fat part of the green toward the hole.

Now you are playing with all of the green and not just the small part where the hole is located.

If you pull the shot a bit, then the ball is right on target; if the shot is pushed or not drawn enough, then it will hit the safe area of the green. Either way, the ball is safely on the green and you are putting instead of chipping for your birdie or par.

This theory also holds true when the pin is on the right, front, or back of the green. No matter where the hole is cut, there is a "fat" part of the putting surface. Always try to start the ball for the safe or big part of the target area, and you will have the odds working for you immediately.

Proper Club Selection

It makes no difference how well you execute a shot if you have made the wrong decision in selecting the club to use.

The most common error, of course, comes in not selecting the proper club for distance.

Experiment on the practice tee with all of your clubs and learn exactly how far you hit each one.

Then, w h e n you play a course for the first time, take a score card and mark off each hole from different places in the fairway—for instance, a tree or sprinkler head—and note those exact distances. Now you have a precise reference point for each hole.

Distances for each club vary, of course, as conditions change. Obviously you must take more club into the wind and less club when the wind is at your back.

Another consideration is the firmness of the greens. Say you have 150 yards to the pin and you usually hit a seven-iron this distance. However, the greens are very firm and the ball is not holding at all. Then you must allow for the roll when the ball hits. Use an eight-iron and let the ball roll the extra 10 yards.

In the Texas Open, I had a chance to win the tournament when I got to the 17th hole. The wind was in my face, and there was trouble in front of the green. It was a seven-iron shot. But I took a six-iron to make sure I had plenty of club. You know the rest. I hit the ball over the green and out of bounds and took a double bogey on the hole.

How to Avoid Trouble

It's obvious your score will suffer if you constantly get into trouble. This not only eliminates any chance you have for a birdie, but also cuts your chance for a par.

There are certain precautions you can use that will keep you out of trouble.

One line of thought advocates aiming at the trouble—for example, trees, traps, creeks, etc.—and hooking or fading the ball away from the trouble. However, if you aren't a professional this is precarious if you can't execute each shot perfectly.

My own idea is to aim the ball away from the trouble and play back toward the obstacle. Give yourself a 100 per cent area of tolerance.

By this, I mean if the trees or creek are on the left, aim to the right and hook the ball toward the trouble. If you feel you can only hook the ball 30 yards to the left, then aim 40 yards to the right and you will never reach the trouble.

There are also times you play it safe to stay out of trouble. At the fourth hole in the Westchester Classic, I noted right away that all the trouble was on the left, while on the right all you had to worry about was a big rock. It was a long hole, but instead of a driver, I used a three-wood off the tee. I couldn't reach the rock, and I had better control to avoid the trouble on the left.

Give yourself a chance to score well—stay out of trouble whenever possible. Don't hit before you think the shot out. Don't just hit and hope!

Planning Your Round

As in football or basketball, you must have a game plan for your golf—an outline that you have devised beforehand and one that you will follow, no matter what is happening in your round.

I generally divide the course into two categories—par holes and birdie holes.

Par holes are those that I only try to par—holes where a bogey is more of a possibility than a birdie. I make doubly sure that I hit the fairway and then hit the safe part of the green and conservatively two-putt for my par—not many birdies here, but no bogeys at all.

The birdie holes are the holes where I can gamble some and still make par if I make a bad shot, usually the par fives and very short par fours where there is no trouble around.

The real key to planning a round is sticking to the plan entirely and without emotion while on the course. Too many times we make a bogey or two, get panicky and start charging and forcing to get these strokes back.

At the PGA one year, I knocked myself out of any possible contention on the 16th hole of the last round by breaking my pattern. Because I felt I had to make up strokes, I got bold.

I was in the right-hand rough on the drive on the par-five hole, where the green is guarded by a lake. The normal procedure would have been to hit it short of the water and pitch over it. I made a play for the pin, which was cut up front, and hit into the lake.

You must play each hole as if it were the only hole you will play all day. Don't let what has happened before or afterward affect your play of any hole.

Playing Out Of Trouble

Until you reach a very advanced stage in your golf game, the key word in escaping from trouble spots is "safety first."

More often than not, higher scores rather than lower ones result from gambling out of tight spots.

Take the safe way home and you'll always make it. Don't make another mistake trying to make up for the first one.

When in trouble and reaching the green is out of the question, your first thought should be to get back onto the fairway—even if you have to shoot backward to do it.

If sometimes you see a professional take the "chicken" way out—believe me, he is playing from experience. There is an unwritten rule among the touring pros which is very simple but makes a lot of sense and saves a lot of money during the year—a double bogey is better than a triple bogey, a bogey is better than a double bogey, and a par is better than a bogey. Don't make it any worse than it already is by using futile heroics.

At the Cleveland Open, on the fifth hole, I hooked my drive off the fairway onto a cart path. There was a creek in front of the green. When I checked the situation, I saw there was a chance of making it with a six-iron, or maybe a seven. But it was a big gamble, even though I needed a par. So I hit a simple wedge shot back to the fairway, then a full nine-iron to the green which left me a 10-foot putt. I sank it and got my par anyway.

When you have a ball buried in a trap or have an impossible pin placement coming from a trap, don't get cute with a shot that even a pro could not execute. Take your bogey and go on to the next hole.

Strategy In the Wind

When playing in blowing breezes, use the wind as an asset—not an irritable hindrance.

The one thing that ruins more shots when the wind is blowing is a loss of balance somewhere during the swing itself.

Because we are the tallest structure around, the wind has a tendency to topple us over and continually keep us off-balance in some manner. This, of course, is compounded by the fact that we are swinging faster and harder to combat the wind and thus lose all of our leverage.

I have much better luck with the wind if I take a little more club and use a shorter, more-compact swing. This keeps everything under control and doesn't give the wind a chance to work on my swing. Never press or force—just swing well within yourself with very compact movements.

Whenever possible, get the ball into the wind. Never let it go with the wind. Then it's at the mercy of the wind and is out of your control.

If the wind is blowing from left to right, you must hook the ball from right to left into the wind. In this way the ball and wind are counteracting forces and the net result is control. Don't fade it unless the wind is from right to left. Don't be afraid of the wind—it can actually be a friend.

Playing In the Rain

Playing in the rain is never any fun and what it can do to your golf game isn't funny, either.

First and most important, keep your grips dry at any cost. I often tell my caddy that I can play if I am wet and I can play if he is wet, but I cannot play if my grips are wet.

Always keep your club well-covered and don't remove the club from the bag until absolutely necessary.

The most trouble when it's raining results from the wet fairways and the soggy wet lies. You get a "flying" shot with absolutely no spin on the ball. It is a very difficult shot to control.

I have more luck with it if I play the ball a bit farther forward in my stance and pick it off the grass cleanly instead of hitting down and through as usual. This shot is not as pretty and has very little spin, but it has a maximum of control under the circumstances and will fill the bill nicely.

I won at Indianapolis in the rain by playing it conservative. On the ninth hole, when I had a bad drive, I didn't panic. It looked like a two-iron to the pin, but I took a four-iron instead on the wet fairway and "flew" the ball 200 yards dead to the middle of the green.

Rain and wet conditions also affect the rolls of your chips and putts to a great extent.

Not only will the ball roll much slower, but the breaks in the greens will not be as acute. Play most of these putts straighter in and hit them more firmly.

116

Making Decisions

Indecision has cost me more money than any other factor in golf. Not making a final decision on which club to hit or the exact line of a putt has even cost me a tournament or two.

You can never make a good pass at any shot if you aren't sure you have the right club; the same holds true with a putt—even more so.

You must decide right away which club you are going to use and convince yourself that it's the right one. And when lining up a putt, look at it from every angle and then immediately decide which way it will break and hit it before you can change your mind.

Indecision can be a most expensive proposition. During the last round of the Greater Hartford Open, I figured that 13-under would win the tournament. I needed a 65. I might have gotten it except that on four of the last five holes, when I had putts of six feet and under for birdies, I missed three of the four. That was the margin I lost by. And the reason I didn't make those putts was that I couldn't decide how the ball was going to break. My own inability to read the green quickly cost me.

Another area that often offers some chance for indecision is the approach to the green. Depending on the pin position, you must decide which club you are going to use and then what shot you will attempt—high, low, hook, fade. It makes no difference—just decide and be positive.

You can never make a free and easy swing with your mind still thinking about which club to use or how the putt will actually break, etc.

Play the Way You Feel

Too many players feel that they are just one kind of player and that it is against the rules to change. They say they are hookers or slicers and that's how they are destined to play—almost as if they were machines incapable of any deviation.

I'd buy it if we were machines. But we wake up on a different side of the bed every day. Always go to the practice tee before you play and hit a few to see just how you feel and how you are actually hitting the ball for this particular day.

You may be a hooker and find this day you are hitting it straight or cannot get your hook to work properly. Take what you wake up with and play with it to the best of your ability.

Ordinarily you might be a very long driver, but on this particular day you feel sluggish or for some reason can't get the club to moving the right speed.

Don't fight it. Just play the way you feel, swing easy, keep the ball in play and make up the difference some place else.

Remember, you're not a repeating machine and you don't hit every shot every day exactly the same. Learn to adjust your thinking with your swing and take each day as it comes because each one will be different.

Playing in Cold Weather

I believe the most difficult playing conditions occur in the winter months when cold weather is p r e v a l e n t. You probably won't be able to get the same results in cold weather that you do in nice warm weather.

However, some of the following tips can improve your cold weather scores.

Obviously, the first thing that will help is to keep warm. Sometimes to keep warm you must wear so many clothes that you can't swing properly.

The pros encounter these conditions frequently, so we simply must buck up to the cold and wear a minimum that won't impede our swing. We carry extra sweaters and jackets to wear when walking or waiting between shots.

A trick of the pros is to carry several extra balls under all the clothing so that they will stay warm, then switch to a warm ball every hole. A ball will respond much better and go farther if it is kept warm. Cold balls have no resiliency and won't always react the same.

Your shafts also lose some whip and kick in cold weather. Therefore, you may have to use more club than normal and swing a bit slower in order to give the shaft a chance to come into play properly.

Don't try for midsummer form and your cold weather play will warm up.

For us on the tour, the Bing Crosby Open in late January generally causes a problem because it usually comes up chilly, the wind off the ocean cutting through you. If you're not careful it can affect your concentration. I take all the precautions mentioned above when the weather dictates it. I also bring hand warmers along to give myself a maximum shot.

Selecting Chip Shot

Too many golfers only have one, or maybe two, chip shots. They use the same club and the same shot from anywhere and under any circumstances.

They obviously don't have the odds working for them when a large variety of short shots are available.

On any chip shot, select the one that will get the ball on the green the quickest way possible.

Always try to hit the green very quickly and get the ball rolling on the surface. Stay away from the more-lofted clubs and use the straighter-faced ones that won't carry as far and will get the ball rolling sooner.

There are times, however, for a high-lofted shot that won't roll at all. They're very difficult to execute and are dangerous for anyone but a professional. These shots should be used to carry a trap and there is very little green between the edge and the pin.

Another very effective chip shot is the "Texas wedge." This is using a putter from off the green.

I highly recommend this type shot whenever possible—especially when the terrain is flat and the grass is not high around the fringe.

On the 18th hole at Pensacola one year, I had to make a par for a 64. I was in back of the green, on an elevation of about four feet. The grass was wet, and the crowd had been back there trampling it down. So I used my putter as a "Texas wedge" and rolled the ball over the hump and down the hill to the pin to salvage my par.

Develop new chip shots around the green so that you'll have more than one shot. Try a little variety and notice the improvement in your short game.

Percentage On the Greens

The hardest lesson that I ever had to learn about putting was that you cannot make every putt on every green every day. There are some putts that are very easy to hole out and others that just should not be attempted.

It's difficult when you have missed a shot and have a long putt for your par to resist the temptation to go for it. However, on these long putts you will three-putt more often than not if you charge recklessly.

There are certain ideas to keep in mind when putting from different angles and disances that will keep you from three-putting.

When putting uphill, always leave the ball short of the hole so that you will have an uphill second putt. If you charge and go by the hole, you then have a tricky downhill putt for your par.

The same holds true for those tricky sidehill putts. If you charge any slick sidehill putt and miss it, you are then going downhill and past the hole before you know what happened.

Before you putt, make a definite decision as to how the putt will break. Then examine the green for any grain and make the proper adjustment.

Finally, decide if your putt is actually a good risk. If so, make a good smooth attempt to hole it. If not, then play it safe and be satisfied with two putts. Once in awhile you may get lucky and find the first one goes in anyway.

That's what happened to me when I won the Tournament of Champions at Las Vegas. I sank a long putt on the final hole to nose out Arnold Palmer.

At the least, two putts would give me a tie. But who wants to take on Palmer in a playoff? There's no percentage in that.

So I went at the hole boldly, but knowing that if I didn't make it, I still had that tie possibility. As luck would have it, the shot was good.

Always Keep on Trying

The most difficult thing to get across to any golfer is to never give up. Always keep trying. You never know when you are going to hole a shot from anywhere on the course.

If you can just keep trying, no matter how badly things are going, things have a way of working out. If you keep on plugging, you can beat most of your opponents b e c a u s e **THEY** will give up w h e n things start to go bad.

When I first started on tour, Jay Hebert gave me a very great lesson. We were playing together and I was having a bad day and was ready to give up and miss the cut. I figured if I barely made the cut what was the difference. I was too far back to win anyway.

Jay told me that in the past 10 years he had made $75,000 in tournaments where he had just barely made the cut—just by not giving up and staying right in there and trying extra hard.

He said everyone else had the same idea that I had, and he just passed them while they were standing around feeling sorry for themselves.

If you keep trying, you won't always come back and win, but at least you'll give yourself some kind of chance. And some chance, even a small one, is better than none.

As you come on, you start to build confidence and change from a defensive to an offensive golfer.

When I was playing head-to-head with Arnold Palmer at Las Vegas, needing a birdie on the last hole to win, I gambled. There is a lake on the right and out-of-bounds on the left. The other rounds I'd been hitting a two-iron safely off the tee, following by a four-wood and a pitch. But this time I took a driver and knocked it right in the middle to put me in good position for the winning birdie.

Psychology, Temperament

I believe a golfer's greatest asset is an even temperament —no ups and no downs. Take everything in stride as if nothing really mattered. You must actually develop an indifferent attitude.

With this more-or-less complacent outlook you can concentrate better on what you are doing now and not on what has happened or what is forthcoming.

You must be only aware of this particular moment—this one shot right now.

Temperament is not an obvious thing.

Jack Nicklaus out on the course looks like nothing could ever bother him. He's built a shell around his feelings, but underneath he's churning just like everybody else. He's simply learned to control them because that's the best way for him.

Arnold Palmer, on the other hand, shows emotion easily. He looks like he's ready to start breaking clubs. But Arnie uses those displays to blow off steam and a second later he's forgotten all about it and gone on to the next shot.

Of course, your concentration also can be interrupted by a particularly good shot. If you made an eagle, you probably would be thinking about it on the next tee and lose sight of the drive coming up.

I play much better with an "I-don't-care" outlook. If I can convince myself that no matter how badly I perform, the world isn't coming to an end, then I play more at ease and with less pressure on each shot.

Relax next time out and don't play each shot as if your life depended on it. Golf that is fun is much easier to play!

What to Do About a Shank

Throughout my years of playing and teaching golf, one question keeps coming up more than all the rest put together: "What can I do about a shank?"

I can tell now when someone's going to ask this question—they always have the most futile and forlorn look on their faces.

Unfortunately, this problem is generally one of loss of confidence and can't be handled with a mechanical change. When you hit one shank, you forever expect the next one and, with this attitude, it'll soon come.

The remedy is to forget your problem, concentrate on executing some kind of "trick" shot on purpose—a hook, slice, etc. It takes your mind off shanking and puts it on something else specific and tangible.

Mechanically speaking, this shank is caused from loss of balance at address. This imbalance results from the player getting up on his toes at address or rocking back on his heels. Either can result in throwing your arc out of kilter.

Maintaining proper balance is important whether your problem is shanking or something else.

You might try to improve your balance when an epidemic of shanking comes around, but the big problem will be confidence. You will be afraid that every shot will be a shank and so be timid with your swing, which in turn causes more shanking.

My best advice, as I said, is to forget your problem and concentrate on some other type of specific shot. Actually try to execute a hook or a slice, and your swing will fall back into place as your confidence returns.

The Press

To begin with, no golf swing should start from a dead stop. A jerky beginning is usually bound for disaster. The forward press is a widely recommended action for beginning a swing and it has no detractors here.

The press, more subtle than overt, triggers the swing. There are several ways to do this, although all produce some kind of motion toward the target.

The most common is a slight movement of the hands toward the flag. If you have  limber, supple hands that move quickly, position them slightly behind the ball at address, then move them forward slightly and start the takeaway immediately.

The Easy Approach

A friend of mine, a teaching pro, was having his usual trouble with a woman golfer. Like so many other people, she was convinced that golf is a complex game. Her mind was crowded with dos and don'ts and no matter how he tried, he couldn't convince her to swing naturally.

Then he noticed a young boy swinging a club nearby. He called the kid over, teed up a ball and asked him to hit it. The boy nonchalantly socked the ball 200 yards down the fairway.

The woman blinked. "What were you thinking about when you hit that ball?" she asked. "Nothing," the boy replied. "Nothing at all."

"But that's impossible," she blurted. "There are a hundred things you have to remember to hit a ball that well."

"Maybe so, lady," the boy said, "but **I don't think of anything. I just swing.**"